Rambled Thoughts

Poems and Other Musings
by
Lee'Ann Imel-Hartford

Namri'd
Publishing, LLC

Namri'd Publishing, LLC
2 Marietta Court Ste A #117
Edgewood, NM 87015

www.namridpublishing.com

Namri'd Publishing, LLC and the Namri'd Publishing logo are Reg.   U.S. Pat. & TM Off.

ISBN-13: 978-0-9985432-2-2
ISBN-10: 0-9985432-2-5

First Printing: November, 2017

10 9 8 7 6 5 4 3 2 1

Printed in the United States of America

To my husband and best friend, may our souls continue to find each other throughout eternity.

To my sister Dawn Marie Imel, 12/29/1955 – 09/07/2017, the inspiration for Dawn Breaks. I will always love you, my beautiful sister. We will meet again someday. Take care of mom.

CONTENTS

WATER

LOVERS' POND

The sounds
of the trickling pond
mesmerized my heart
and caused me to dream.
His love forever cast.

My mind floats
over time and space
through oceans and continents
searching for memories of him.
His love forever cast.

He is waiting
on the bridge
in the city
in the forest.
His love forever cast.

The sounds
of the trickling pond
bring me to the present.
I see him standing there.
His love forever cast.

WAVES

Crashing into me
pushing me into the sand
pulling me up to the surface
my flailing legs and arms.
Drowning

Floating body, churning waves
water flows
giving and taking life

The waves push me back up
the surface welcomes me
I gasp for air
the salty sea chokes me.
Living

OCEAN TIDES

The ocean tides call to those
whose souls need fed
by their calming water

The ocean tides call to every living creature
providing nourishment
and gentle loving arms

The ocean tides call to God
hoping that life will continue
throughout the centuries

The ocean tides call to me
like a mother calling her child
I want to go home

CRYSTAL POOL

The crystal pool sparkles in the sunlight
calling me into its cool waters
I float, mind wandering, as the water pulls
me to and fro

The sun warms my body
as the water cools from below

My skin burns and turns red
water droplets glisten on my body
and cool my hot skin

I hear my name
but I just keep floating

The water is my cocoon
it keeps me safe
and sheltered from the world

FLOOD

The great flood of hate envelopes the earth
as if God's light has left His children to fend
for themselves

Words flood the stratosphere
Hurting labels create divide

Speak only the truth as "they" see it
your opinion never matters

God's light returns
as water washes clean

No more labels
No more hate

THE LITTLE WHITE GAZEBO

We sat at the edge of the beach
just alongside the foliage
under the little white gazebo

The sound of the ocean waves
breaking on the shore
was mesmerizing

The salt filled air
warms my skin
soft breezes cool

My lips were salty
quenched by a sweet rum punch

Little silver fish swam by playfully
joyfully jumping out of the water

The little neighborhood cat
runs friskily across the sand
searching for little morsels

Hours pass by slowly
lulling me to sleep
dreaming of splendor

The sun sets along the horizon
signaling the end
of another beautiful day

GOLDENEYE

Beautiful beaches
calling me home

Waves break on shore
lulling me to dream
of an era gone by

Soft breezes calling me
to scribe my heart

Palms sway
to the beat of heaven's music
as the waves keep time

Clouds glide across the sky
creating a palette that spurs the imagination

The scent of lemongrass fills the air
saltwater pools soothe burnt skin
sand tickles my toes

Soft music plays
the local sounds of love

I feel the presence of him
the one who walked these shores
his gifts forever bringing joy

His voice echoes in the wind
secret whispers shared inspire me

Oh how I long to return
to the home of words
that carry me away

SEASONS

SNOW IN APRIL

The earth, still tired from winter's drought
struggles to breathe and grow

The brown ground searches to quench thirst
no water in sight

The earth needs a reprieve
creatures search for food and comfort

The sun attempts to warm the earth
but midnight frost harkens

April snow showers lull God's children
by bringing spring sleep

The flora and fauna
feel the warmth of the sun

The snow melts
and provides needed drink

NEW MEXICO WINDS

The winds howl
pushing flowers, leaves
dust blowing

The wind ushers in spring
calling animals from their slumber
flowers bloom

The wind dries the land
and ushers in the spring
hope for summer beckons

The wind lessens
as the heat of summer looms
only to return come fall

FRAIL SPRING BLOOMS

The frail spring blooms
thirst for the life of summer
never lasts
yet is reborn

SUMMER HEAT

The summer heat knows no bounds
dry, thick, choking air
water quenches not

Cool summer sheets
bring reprieve

As ice melts on hot skin
lovers paint their bodies

Sweat drops lay on skin
bodies entwined
sex caused sleep

EARTH'S CYCLE

Spring to wake
my earth child
enjoy the fresh nectar

Summer heat
brings weary flora
searching for last drops

Fall to sleep my little ones
gather nourishment
prepare for slumber

Winter's dormancy looms
rest my earth child
till spring returns anew

ECHOES

The wind carries the echoes
of your voice calling me
from throughout the centuries

WILDFIRE

The orange haze of smoke fills the air
it chokes the life from flora and fauna

Was it a careless man?
A senseless act?

Thousands flee
leaving their homes
looters take advantage

What shall become of love and life?
Will we have hope again?
Or shall doom ever follow?

THE SUMMER BREEZE

The summer breeze
carries the morning birdsong
awakens me from slumber

The summer breeze
smells of sweet nectar
flowers sway

The summer breeze
upon the water
reminds me of you

The summer breeze
feels warm against my skin
your hands follow my curves

The summer breeze
fills my mind with sweet memories
of love, lust, you

WARRIORS

GOD BLESS THE WARRIORS

God bless the warriors
who fight for their country
with distinction, honor, and glory

They sacrifice love, life, and happiness
so that you may be free

But what do you do with that freedom?
You sacrifice it by acting petty

You voice hate in the name of free speech
the speech that our blessed warriors
fought and died for

Yes, God bless the warriors
so that your true self is free

NIGHT WATCH

I gird myself
ready for battle
to protect the one I love

The night watch marches through the gates
that protects my love from harm

He waits
for my return

I run into his arms
and he removes my armor
that conceals my womanhood

No one can know my identity
I am woman, fierce and loyal

I protect you, my love
from all that is evil
I am your warrior, your lover

BEAUTIFUL WARRIOR

Beautiful warrior
loves with all her soul
but always hides
behind her armor

She wears a coat
of maille and leather
but it cannot protect
her tender heart

Her black Friesian
carries her weight
but cannot support
the loss she feels

What untold secrets
does this beauty
and her beast hide
behind their armor?

Only love from one
with a pure heart
can save this lost soul
from the burden of herself

LOVE'S BATTLE

I fight for you
my love never wanes

Through the bastion of my love
I ready my weapon to protect you
from those who seek to do you harm

I fight for you
my love never falters

I seek justice from those
who try to come between us
my blade is swift

I fight for you
my love never ends

THE HEAVENS

DUSK

The dusk
envelops me like a cancer
calling me back into oblivion

But I wait for you
the one that haunts me
throughout eternity

SUNSET

The sunset is a mystery
waiting to be discovered

The sun's beams
bleed into oblivion
and melt into the sea

As the sun passes the horizon
the night looms
calling lovers

Stars peek out
ever getting brighter
romance builds

Night sounds bloom
calling lust

HEAVEN BOUND

Love throws itself
falling through the heavens
sanctuary lost

Centuries pass
love travels throughout the galaxy
searching for home

The journey comes to an end
love no longer exists
the angels call love home

God's kiss forever gone
love's corpse buried
eternity lost

NIGHT SKIES

Black cloth
covered dome
pricked holes
allow light through

Stars
moonscape night
shadows play
wolves howl

Lovers' lane
voices moan
pleasure abound
sleep

SUNBURST

Her love was a sunburst
burning bright across the heavens

DAWN BREAKS

Dawn breaks
rays come together
the rain falls
sadness

Days go by waiting for light
we fight for hope

Black skies fill the days and nights
we pray for a new day

Light
skies fill with joy
rays beam bright

But the light was short
and darkness returned

Rays come together again
searching for the light that is not there

The light has returned to whence it came
forever smiling down upon the rays

SEARCHING THE HEAVENS

My soul stays afloat
wandering the sea of heaven
as God searches for a body
for me to inhabit

I search through the stars
longing for a place
to call home

The beautiful planets call to me
but I do not answer.
I am looking for you.
I wait for you to call

Angels sing
God has found me a place
that place is with you

MORNING'S ANGEL

Morning's angel watches over me
protecting me from the earth's evils
she prepares me for the battles of the day
ensuring I am at peace and feel secure

Morning's angel is always with me
she is love, caring, peace
she eschews hate
and battles my demons

Morning's angel protects the ones I love
she watches them and keeps harm at bay
her fire is as if armor
as she fights against hate, greed, and pain

Morning's angel watches over me
until the day ends and I take my last breath
she follows me throughout eternity
protecting me, loving me, honoring me

MORNING SUN

The morning sun peers from behind the
clouds
it warms the earth and strengthens its flora
and fauna

As the day progresses
light makes silhouettes

We ask ourselves, what hides behind the
shadows
what mysteries lie beyond

As night draws neigh
creatures of the dark emerge

The moon takes hold of the atmosphere
until the morning sun arises again

ETERNITY

SOULS BLOOM ETERNAL

Spring roses bloom
To grace the lovers' tomb
Millennia passes
Hands held through time
Souls meet eternally

As souls bloom through the centuries
Lovers lost
Hope renews the lust
Ever wandering
Searching, wanting

Searching for lovers' bloom
Love fades and withers
Death casts shadows
Bodies turn to dust
The wind stirs

The wind of fate shall bloom again
Lovers meet, always wanting
Souls eternal
Lovers embrace
Always searching, always wanting

PURPLE FLOWERS

Oh how I love purple flowers
Is it because I have loved them
across time and space?

When did they capture my heart?
Why do they speak to me?
To my soul eternal

Was it the Columbine I saw
near the Stamford Bridge in 1066
when I first saw you?

Was it the Thistle in the fields of Scotland
where we fought together during
battles in the Scottish Highlands?

The Crocus near Poenari Castle?
They seem to call us back
as if we are destined to open history

Or the Iris
vast along the castles of Germania
symbols of lust and wanting?

Or was it the Bougainvillea
in the first bouquet you gave me

during this life time?

Purple flowers are my heart
I feel them always in my soul
Just as you are my heart and soul

ETERNAL LOVE

How do you define love that follows you throughout eternity?

Is it part of your soul? Or is it something that you just know and cannot describe?

Do you have memories of your love?

Does he haunt your days and nights?

Is he sitting right beside you through thick and thin?

There is no way that I know to describe eternal love, except that I would be nowhere without him.

WANDERLUST

I wander time and space
I search for love lost
And love found

Egyptian tombs
Mars
Venus

I travel the centuries
Planets hold no bounds
Dimensions are nothing

I wander time and space
Always searching
Always wanting

BEGINNINGS

The tale begins
1066 Stamford Bridge
Battle fierce

We travel the centuries
Searching for love
Lost in time

Planets fall
And rise while we search
Through time and space

The tale ends with my soul
Ever searching for yours
Loving you always

DARE TO DREAM

Dare to dream of lovers past
Searching for his soul
Is he on the bridge?
Down by the sea?
Searching, wanting

Dare to dream of lovers past
Holding hands
Silent whispers
Bodies glisten
Searching, wanting

Dare to dream of lovers past
Wandering time
Warriors, lovers
Traversing time and space
Searching, wanting

WHAT IFS

Thinking about what ifs
Always wanting
Never doing

Do I have the courage
to fulfill my dreams?

Or am I lost
searching for something perfect?
That may never come my way

Bucket list incomplete
a sad death

ETERNAL SOUL

I believe our souls are eternal
when you find your soul mate
you will travel throughout eternity
constantly looking for them.

It's just a matter of finding
each other again.

THE CHASE

The thrill of the chase
wandering through time
searching for you

There were times
I did not know you
but somehow felt your presence

There were times
you did not know me
but I chased you anyway

We are meant to be
we will always chase each other
until we chase no more

MEMORIES

The memories of you will haunt me throughout all eternity. I will always love and need you. You are my twin flame. Our lives cannot be without the other.

I will always remember you no matter where my soul's journey takes me next.

TIME

Throughout time I search for you
The one I saw centuries ago on the bridge
I will never forget you

Time will always be on my side
As I search the galaxy through time and
space
I will never forget you

We only have time, you and I
Passing each other throughout many
dimensions
I will never forget you

Will this be the last time are souls are
together?
Or do we have one more chance
I will never forget you

THE PATH

He crosses her path
throughout the centuries
she ever watchful

The two unite
passion ensues
only to fade away
as bodies turn to dust

Passing through eternity
they will meet again

Will he remember
her beauty and
the love they share?

Time passes
she never forgets
the yearning that haunts her

The love they share
keeps them on the path
always searching for signs
of the hunger that binds them

NEVER RESTING

I will forever chase you
throughout the centuries
never resting

I will seek your beautiful soul
longing to touch it
never resting

I will long to hold your body
close to mine forever
never resting

I will die with you in my arms
the wind will take my bones
never resting

I will forever chase you
throughout the centuries
never resting

I CLAIM YOUR HEART

I search for you throughout the centuries
to claim the heart that I love

Your body ever changes
but your soul remains the same

I never know if it is you
but I keep searching for the heart that I
claim

I will wander the valleys and the mountains
of this world and the next

Searching for the heart that belongs to me
the one that ever searches for me

I will search forever until your soul sings to
me
the song of our love

SOULS

My body cannot contain my soul
for my soul is a being without limits

My soul traverses space and time
searching for a love that is timeless

My love for you will never wane
as I search for the body that contains your
soul

Our souls are meant to be together
one cannot live without the other

WISTFUL SOUL

My wistful soul
will search for you
ever longing; searching

Note

As you may have surmised, this collection of poems is very personal and has much to do with the journey of the soul and the past lives we, my lover and I, have lived. It is our journey across time and space so much as we have been able to construct through historical research. We take hope that there is more to life; that our souls are eternal and connected to other souls despite time and distance numbering billions of miles and across countless centuries. This is only a part of our story, our love. What may lay buried deep is lost to our minds. I hope you have enjoyed these readings and hope that it has brought you hope, love, and faith in some small way. Be blessed and go forth, knowing that there is so much more to all of this; that we are greater than this.

About the Author

Lee'Ann Imel-Hartford has a Doctor of Business Administration in Homeland Security Leadership and Policy. She spent over 21 years in the United States Air Force traveling the world and getting into trouble. She currently lives in New Mexico with her husband and furbabies and has aspirations of retiring at the beach.

Available Now from Namri'd Publishing

2198: A Memoir from the Second Revolution
A novel by Brian Dennis Hartford with Lee'Ann Imel-Hartford

Set in the near future, 2198: A Memoir from the Second Revolution is an uncompromising, often gritty and explosive look into the lives of Benjamin and Lena Bradford as they join and fight as shadow warriors in the world's newest and most powerful Private Military Security Corporation, Paradigm, in a race to defeat both foreign and domestic threats as America, and the world, falls into economic and political chaos. Driven by the desire to hold onto the life they are slowly losing and patriotism for the country they love, they take up arms for an ideal that may no longer exist.

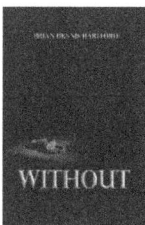

Without
A Novel by Brian Dennis Hartford

A Vampire Novel that Changes Everything

What is forever anyways? To anyone? Ianthe Gold is a Vampire who will do anything to save her one true love, Charlotte Bell Aberdeen. To finally be united with a love that she has been chasing over the millennia, through time and space. Now, she has found the chance to reunite with Charlotte and keep her promise of forever that she had made to her, the soul within, so long ago. But God, as always, has other plans.

WITHOUT, is an epic journey set in the modern day. It eloquently and boldly captures both the beauty and the horror of life, this cosmic journey of the flesh, and the soul within God's grand design. Gritty, ugly, and languishing are just a few emotions evoked as we witness the rise and fall of life and love.

www.ingramcontent.com/pod-product-compliance
Lightning Source LLC
Chambersburg PA
CBHW032112040426
42337CB00040B/269